W0010272

HAPPINESS

the feel-good factor

HAPPINESS

the feel-good factor

Libby Willis
Illustrated by Debbie Lush

**Andrews McMeel
Publishing**

Kansas City

introduction

Some are born happy, some achieve
happiness, and some have happiness thrust
upon them. But the essential, joyous thing is that
everyone can be happy. We don't need to pass exams,
earn a pop star salary, have a model's figure, or win a competition.
It's a gloriously democratic, unifying force: we each feel happy for
our own special reasons and in our own unique way, but happiness
unites us with every human being. It dissolves barriers of country,
creed, race, age, class, and culture. It's a universal emotion, with
an international language—a smile and a laugh are understood
all over the world.

Happiness can be unlooked for, alighting on us out of the blue
from something outside—a letter, good news, a snatch of music.
Or it can flow from a dream coming true at last—a job offer,
recovery from illness, a prayer answered. Something sublime can
send us soaring—an exquisite painting, sunlight breaking through
clouds, hang-gliding over snow-capped mountains—but so can

something incredibly simple, like a tiny flower or a shiny hairdo. Other people can shower us with happiness by a kind word or gesture or just by being themselves. The wonder, beauty, and pure perfection of happiness make us want to treasure every second of it and hug it to us so we never forget it.

Happiness transforms us. It is healing, restorative, rejuvenating, and energizing. It makes us reach for the stars, climb mountains, think big, dare to be different, go for it. It makes us luminous, shining a torch for others in darkness. It makes us more loving and compassionate. The more we share our happiness—giving it away with spendthrift smiles—the more we have ourselves. For "the way to be happy is to make others so."

Sometimes happiness bursts upon us: a sudden, electrifying ecstasy that sends us over the moon. A tingling, tutti-frutti, ticker-tape thing, euphoria that makes us effervescent. But this sort of rapture comes and goes. There is another kind of happiness that steals upon us slowly, and softly permeates our whole being, a warm splendor that suffuses us as wine blushes water. This is the lasting joy that is independent of external circumstances and events—an eternal flame that can never be extinguished. If we have this happiness at our core, we can accept the unacceptable and face whatever comes, with equanimity and courage. It brings a serenity beyond price, a contentment that is not about getting what we want but in wanting what we've got.

This quiet but unshakable joy radiates from those who make the brave decision to be happy, however illogical or irrational. Deep-rooted happiness comes not so much from what happens to us in life as from how we perceive what happens, how we react to it, and what we make of it. It is not the result of a trouble-free life: often the truly happiest

people are those who have
been through immense struggles
and ordeals, and endured intense
pain, suffering, or grief. They rejoice in
life for its own sake, seeing everything as
a gift, looking for the positive in every
situation. With this new vision they see
beauty and worth in the ordinary and find
happiness in the everyday. Even when it's raining,
they can still think, "What a wonderful world." There is
a holiness in this happiness, for it seems heaven sent. It is a
blessing and a state of grace.

best-laid plans

Fabulous, freewheeling happiness is everything being hunky-dory. When once in a while our best-laid plans go perfectly right. When the irreplaceable watch we had lost is returned to us by an honest stranger. When the very last pair of those silver stilettos turns out to be exactly our size. Happiness is finding the pesky jigsaw piece with the emerald edge and part of the sky and the top of the flag. It is waking to find the migraine has gone. The hardly daring to believe it when we've hoped and hoped against all odds and, impossibly, our prayers are answered. It is the heart-bursting joy of a homecoming and a hundred yellow ribbons round the old oak tree.

so lucky in love

L ove is our most sustaining and sublime source of happiness. That out of all the millions of people on earth two of them should meet, recognize in the other their soul mate, and live together in an ever-deepening mutual love is something so miraculous and phenomenal that it seems truly a gift from heaven. Virginia Woolf expressed the awe we feel when, after many years of marriage, she asked a friend,

"What do you think is probably the happiest moment in one's whole life?" Her friend recalled that she continued on, with a "very quiet radiance in her voice, 'I think it is the moment when one is walking in one's garden, perhaps picking off a few dead flowers, and suddenly one thinks: My husband lives in that house—and he loves me.' Her face shone as I had never seen it."

living and forgiving

Holding on to hurts and grudges holds us back from happiness. If we can forgive wrongs as soon as they are said or done, they will flow away as drops off a duck's back, but if we let them stick they stain our joy, covering us with a thick black tar that corrodes and cripples. Letting go of angers, resentments, rejection, and disappointments, we are set free to fly. It makes everything better, not bitter. Being reconciled with someone restores radiance to life —we gain a new friend or regain an old one. Sending rays of love and peace from our hearts to theirs, and smiling whenever we meet them, can lead to hostility being vanquished by harmony and hugs.

shining examples

Some of us come into the world trailing clouds of glory: happy, shiny people with a joie de vivre and a sunny disposition. They glow with a special aura. Some of us come with darker clouds with only the faintest silver lining. We have to work harder at being happy and recognizing rainbows. Perhaps the sun-kissed people, with their warm hearts and helping hands, are here to give us piggyback rides out of the shadows and into the marvelous light.

with an open heart

Happy people are walking welcome mats. If we're always open to new things, blessings come tumbling over the threshold. With an open mind we can be inspired by new ideas and influences. We appreciate the art in an unmade bed. With open ears we hear echoes of laughter and are moved to tears by a teenage band's tune. Holding out a friendly hand, we can tingle

at the touch of the lover we have longed for. With an open heart, love pours in as prodigiously as we give it away. Open eyes spot a golden opportunity and light up at serendipity. Opening up to life, we notice the flame in the icicle and kneel before the burning bush. We find good in unexpected places, talents in unexpected people—and the grace to tell them so.

diamonds are forever

Friends are a girl's best diamonds. They are always on hand to share special moments and dispense their precious pearls of wisdom. Their love is rock solid. They like us whether we are thick or thin and stick with us through huffs and hissy fits. They do not ask us to be flawless, yet they themselves have hearts of gold. They do not need a crystal ball to read our minds. They console and comfort when our world falls apart, and spoil us with fifty-carat kindness. They celebrate with us when we feel like Miss World, putting rings on our fingers and bells on our toes and giving us the full red-carpet treatment. Happiness with them is the real multifaceted genuine thing.

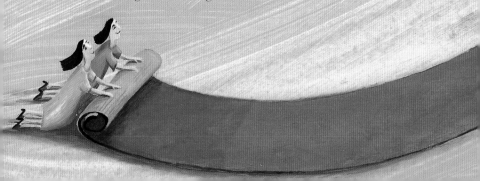

a change of view

Whoosh! All it takes is a single turn of the kaleidoscope and suddenly the world looks completely different—an amazing technicolor place. The idea of change may seem scary, but the rewards can be absolutely scrumptious. Stuck in a groove, we don't feel groovy, but daring to go off on a different track can be the start of a magical mystery tour through life. Change brings a whole new perspective, altering the way we see ourselves and others. "We have to be the changes we want to see in the world" was Gandhi's way of putting it. It can begin with something small—a new haircut, a new hobby —which, like turning the wheel of an ocean liner, slowly sets us on a happier course. Or it can be a supernova seismic thing turning wilderness to wonderland.

give and let live

True happiness is not about what we receive but about what we give. About wanting to make others happy—even at the cost of our own happiness. "If you want others to be happy," said the Dalai Lama, "practice compassion. If you want to be happy, practice compassion." When the lights go out, it isn't easy to be the one who ventures off in search of candles. The greatest happiness comes from not walking by on the other side, from throwing even one starfish back in the sea. To live in such a way that everyone who meets us leaves us feeling happier is a daunting challenge, but is the secret of the happiest people on earth.

happy ever laughter

Happiness sometimes bursts out laughing. Whether we giggle, guffaw, or chortle, laughter genuinely is the best medicine: it triggers the release of endorphins, the body's feel-good hormones, and strengthens our immune system. The seventy thousand or more members of Laughter Club International are seriously funny: dedicated to "health and world peace through laughter," they do breathing and chuckling exercises to counter life's stress and sadness. Seeing the funny side of life helps us tap into happiness, especially if we can laugh at ourselves. And spreading our happiness is heavenly: "He who makes his companions laugh deserves Paradise."

creature comforts

Pets are Prozac on paws. It's official—pets are sometimes taken into hospitals to cheer up patients and speed their recovery. Animals seem to have a hotline to happiness, perhaps because they have a different sense of time, taking each day as it comes and not worrying about the future. They welcome the pleasures that each hour brings and share their moods with us. Rhythmically stroking a silken rabbit relaxes us to serenity, a devoted dog bounding to meet us at the door fills us with joy, and cats are catalysts of quiet delight—they can always find the warmest or sunniest spot on a gray day, and, whether snoozing in our lap or milking every moment of a stupendous stretch, they ooze contentment. Happiness is a velvet purr weaving between our ankles.

a little rain must fall

When the chips are down it's all right to be a couch potato. When we feel low we need the luxury of time to wallow, watching a weepie film with a box of tissues. Rare insights can come on our darkest days, for sometimes what is happening in the shadows is more significant than what is going on in the sunlight. In our own sadness we can sense the sadness of others all over the world and feel a compassionate kinship with them. When blue skies seem a long way off, we can still look for the beauty in raindrops, the shapes in the clouds; we can still keep faith in the idea of sunshine. As we patiently wait in our chrysalis of sadness, a butterfly of happiness will be slowly forming, to unfurl its wings on a wonderful day.

salon days

A day of pampering is a hamper full of happiness. A pedicure treats us to twinkly toes and makes us feel fortunate to have our feet. A manicure gives us the softest hands for holding with our lover and helping those in need. A facial bestows a beautiful glow and puts a fresh complexion on life. A massage makes all our muscles relax and reminds us of the healing power of touch—we sometimes forget that a hug or a squeeze of the hand can mean so much, bringing a smile to a sad face. And an Ayurvedic shirodhara is simply the ultimate in bliss. As a warm stream of herbal oil is poured on our forehead, worries simply melt away. Peace and happiness return when oil is poured on troubled waters.

no place like home

Every room contains a different happiness. The kitchen is cozy and a whistling kettle makes generous mugs of tea for everyone who calls. Puppies play under an old pine table, mellow with memories of merry meals and carved with lovers' hearts. The sitting-room armchairs are deep and dimpled, divine for dozing and daydreaming. On every surface are never-fading smiles in silver frames. Higgledy-piggledy in the hall are hats and coats contented after a country ramble. A telephone trills with a hoped-for call and a letter sealed with kisses slips through the flap. Bliss enfolds us in the bathroom, sanctuary of solitude. Fluffy towels wrap us in a cocoon of calm after a floppy-limbed soak in scented suds. In the hushed haven of a lamp-lit bedroom we snuggle down under feathery quilts and drift into delightful dreams.

natural happiness

Children seem plugged into happiness. They see the world through wondering eyes and marvel at the simplest things—a soap bubble, a rubber duck, the crumpled brown paper surrounding a parcel. Yet as we grow older we tend to lose that wonderment and endless curiosity; our enthusiasm and energy ebb. Happiness is such a natural, unaffected thing that sophistication, cynicism, and irony can make it feel inferior and creep into a corner. To coax it back we may need to regain our child's-eye view of life. To wake up and look at the world as if seeing it for the very first time. To be stunned that the sun rises every morning, that flowers bloom, that we are alive.

summer loving

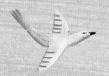

Four seasons, and so many reasons to be cheerful. Spring gambols in with newborn lambs and cheeps with farmyard chicks. Powder puffs of blossom on cherry trees. An impulse from a bluebell wood. Damselflies darting on dappled ponds. An Easter bonnet full of hope. Summer beams in smiling slices of watermelon on picnics in strawberry fields. Croquet on fresh-mown grass. Seagulls bob on sparkling waves as donkeys in straw hats amble along the sand. Armfuls of sunflowers and not enough vases for August. Autumn trundles in with a wheelbarrow heaped with harvest goods and swallows perched on telephone wires. Blackberrying juicily in bramble lanes and dreaming of steaming pies. October shiny with crisp blue skies. Golden groves unleaving. Gusts of wind to fly a kite in stubble fields. Winter crackles cheerfully in an applewood log fire and melts in a doily snowflake. Hills tucked up under a fluffy white quilt. A sleigh ride to the tinkle of reindeer bells. Plum-pudding stirring and mince pies for tea. An angel on a candlelit tree.

think pink

Happiness is tickled pink. It glows in a glass of rosé wine and tints a sliver of Turkish delight slipped between just-kissed lips. It blooms in a posy of pinks picked for a maiden aunt. It pirouettes in a first pair of peach pointe shoes. Woven into a friendship bracelet, it is the cyclamen silk at the center. It sticks its tongue out to one side as it cuts out a lopsided Mother's Day card with pinking shears. Happiness grins at the littlest piglet that no one thought could ever pull through yet survives through a vigil of feeding and love. It looks out through the rose-tinted lenses that lessen headaches. It blushes when it is asked out on a date. It lingers in lipstick on a porcelain cup, a memento of the moment when she said yes.

truly, madly, deeply

The best pick-me-up on a bad-hair day is to really let our hair down. Casting off our inhibitions, we can tingle again with the talent we had as children to be truly, madly, deeply happy. We can feel again that sheer sherbet excitement of whizzing helter-skelter down the hill on a sled. Doing something gloriously zany brings back that zip-a-dee-doo-dah feeling. Maybe we'll play a didgeridoo, maybe we'll go skinny-dipping. Maybe we'll yodel from a treetop, maybe we'll join a pom-pom team. At the end of a crazy paving path is a bouncy castle of happiness.

eternal flame

Choosing to be happy takes courage. After the searing loss of a loved one, happiness can seem far behind us in the past and forever beyond us in a frozen future. Yet happiness is never extinguished; faint and flickering, it endures in a tiny corner of every broken heart. It lights our way forward more healingly than time. Perhaps only by knowing profound sorrow

can we know profound joy. If we can will ourselves to reach
out to happiness and fan it with our love, the flame will grow
stronger and higher, to be set on a windowsill to shine out for
the one who has gone. When we feel ready, we can pick up our
world gently again, like a paperweight snow scene, and see
everything come to life.

feathered friends

While we cannot prevent the birds of sadness flying over our heads, an ancient Chinese proverb says we can stop them from nesting in our hair. Perhaps we may make an aviary in our heart for birds of happiness instead. A bluebird to wake us with joy each morning, and an owl to hoot at night, soothing us to restful slumber. An eagle that rides on the wings of the wind, and a robin resilient through black-ice days. A phoenix rising from ashes of despair and a partridge in a pear tree. A dove with peace in its gentle beak.

picking up the pieces

Life is full of happy accidents, though they may not seem so at the time. Life can pull the rug from under our feet and calamities rain down on our heads. But if we put up an umbrella of hope and muster strength to start afresh unexpected things can happen. While we fumble around on all fours we may discover a four-leafed clover, and looked at from a different angle obstacles turn into stepping-stones that lead us to a yellow-brick road. Dreams may be shattered, but something in the way the fragments fall can spark a visionary gleam we would not otherwise have had. Picking up the pieces, with nothing to lose, we begin to make a magic mosaic and joyously feel whole again.

the pleasure principle

Sadness ambushes us, but happiness embraces us. Sometimes we are afraid to yield to it, feeling we don't deserve it. But happiness is a gift to be welcomed and enjoyed to the full while it lasts. Being happy to the best of our ability is a way of giving thanks and praise. Happiness invites us into the ice-cream parlor of life, in all its sundae glory.

universal joy

Gazing up at the glowing galaxies of a night sky, we can be gathered up into a kind of cosmic happiness. Diamonds sparkling on black velvet, stars dazzle us with their delicate beauty, diffused down to us through hundreds of light-years. They can fill us with an awed awareness of being a tiny part of the universe, and, like a star with its special place in an intricate constellation, connected with those that surround it, being similarly linked to and loved by our family and friends. If ever we feel meaningless or superfluous, it is comforting to think that no artist makes a single brush stroke, word, or note that is not necessary to the perfection of the whole—we are just as needed, here for a reason, in the great scheme of things.

fun and games

Surprise! Surprise! When the lights flick on
in a darkened room and grinning friends spring from
behind the sofa, joy jumps up like a jack-in-the-box. We feel
bubblier than any vintage champagne, floatier than a bunch of
balloons. But all the streamers and banners and cocktails and
congas are really the icing on the cake: What fills us with a dazed
delight is the realization that we are liked. That people have gone
to incredible lengths and conspired in top-secret subterfuge to
prepare a party purely for us. And that thought is ours to cherish
in our take-home bag long after the very last cork has popped.

sweet clarity

If cleanliness is next to godliness, it is a hair's breadth away from happiness, too. A holy happiness comes from a clean conscience. Doing what we know to be right or not succumbing to temptation tests our strength of character but instills us with true tranquillity. Standing up to be counted, we grow in grace; holding back from jumping on a bad bandwagon, we stay rooted on the side of good. When our inner space is pure and

free as Alpine air, we are not upset by people entering our
external personal space and are happy to give others
freedom—we do not try to control, manipulate, or impose
our will on them. If the windows of our soul are as clear as
a glacier mint, we look outward at others and are happy in
their happiness. A chaste mind is a shining chalice to receive
"a white, celestial thought."

kindhearted

When we do a spontaneous act of kindness, happiness will boomerang back to us. It doesn't have to be a grand gesture—just a little, unlooked-for gift; a simple thank-you to someone who is rarely thanked; carrying a stranger's heavy case; an hour of tea and sympathy with a lonely neighbor. Kindness costs nothing but is priceless to those we give it to. A compassionate thought or deed, when completely selfless and not hoping for any return, will bless us with happiness, too.

the beach joys

Does happiness roll in with the waves? Life is a beach to be explored and we gather wisdom there like shells swept in by the tide. Storm-tossed and slate gray one day, tranquil and turquoise the next, the sea is as changeable as our lives, reminding us that calm will follow the tempests we go through. Strolling among rock pools, we catch our reflection and come face to face with our true selves. Surfing in on the crest of a wave, the sun hot on our skin, we feel the surfboard firm beneath our feet and delight at our skill in controlling it. Exhilaration and freedom energize us like the bracing air.

Gliding in to safety, we bask in a new-found sense of achievement from having bravely ridden the waves and left fears far out at sea. Sitting amid the windswept sand dunes, we may see our failings in a different light. "To measure yourself by your smallest deed is to reckon the power of the ocean by the frailty of its foam."

little by little

We cannot all trek to the South Pole or stand on the crest of Everest. Yet there is heroism in a humdrum life that demands a daily secret struggle. Every person has a vocation and the courage needed to fulfill it can be greater when it lacks any grandeur. Investing drudgery with delight gilds it with an aureole: "Work is love made visible." We know an oboe happiness then, soulful, enduring, poignant, pure. Sometimes simply keeping on keeping on is an epic journey, yet a succession of little successes amount to a tremendous triumph. Facing up to a paralyzing fear, achieving a goal after countless failures, we are swept off our feet with a somersaulting joy and zoom on a comet right over the moon.

what a relief

We do not have to be good at everything. It was Einstein who said, "Do not worry about your difficulties in mathematics; I assure you that mine are greater." Struggling to be superwoman or superman seldom leaves us feeling super. It can be a tremendous relief to accept that there is such a word as can't and that to admit it isn't defeatist. A tree is happy to be a tree even though it will never

swing from its own branches. We each have our own particular
talents. An ugli fruit is small and saddled with an off-putting
name, yet it tastes exquisitely sweet. Serenity comes
from finding out what we really can't do and
rejoicing in what we can—then doing it with
all our heart and soul.

in the nature of things

Nature invites us to have a field day. Being out in the open air makes our hearts and minds expand and is a breath of fresh air to weary spirits. Nature is a golden notebook with wisdom and beauty on every page, open for us to immerse ourselves in. Time stands still on the top of a mountain as we watch a condor circling below us, bearing our troubles away on its wings. The vastness of a prairie puts our problems in perspective, the bounce of a kangaroo puts a spring in our step. Immensity in an iceberg, intricacy in an insect's eye. Thunder and lightning split the skies, just as our own lives crash and flash, but after the storm comes the still small voice in a world now hushed and daisy fresh. Sitting beneath a magnolia tree we can hear the grass singing and the squirrel's heartbeat and petals of peace drift to our feet.

the happy hour

What is the happiest time of day? The earliest hours, when morning gilds the skies and blackbirds dip their beaks in dewdrops? Or midday, when the sun blazes overhead and a shepherd rests on a Greek hillside, unpacking his lunch of home-baked bread and a chunk of goat's cheese, washed down with water from a shimmering stream? Perhaps it is at four o'clock, when children skip home from school and proudly present a splotchy painting. Or is it at twilight, when, wandering among sleepy borders, cradling a basket of fresh-picked roses, we hear the soft notes of a Chopin nocturne?

flower power

Unhappy gardeners are thin on the ground. There is something about being tillers of the soil that earths us and soothes the soul. Planting bulbs, sowing seeds, taking cuttings, potting in the shed: each has its particular pleasure. We know the patient happiness of daily tending and watering, watching and waiting for a delicate flower to bloom against all odds. Getting down and dirty in the vegetable patch is guaranteed to lift us up: Nothing beats a dose of double-digging for working out frustration. And a spot of weeding is a wonderful way to weed out negative thoughts that may have taken root in our minds and brought unhappiness. Sharing tips and giving away cuttings, we discover the joy of being perennially generous. Everything isn't always rosy in the garden—as in life, we come up against thorns or are plagued by disappointments that descend like blackflies—but there are always consolations. Something is always flowering somewhere. Even in the dead of winter a single snowdrop can make our heart sing. Gardeners are happy with what they have; they realize that, while the grass may look greener on the other side, it could turn out to be AstroTurf.

art and soul

Happiness draws out the latent creativity in all of us. It throws up a ball and our imagination leaps to catch it. We dream dreams and see visions, hear unheard melodies, and hold our breaths as we make them reality. At times we feel a gay abandon, splashing our lives with color and action; at others peace pervades us. Life spreads before us as a fluid canvas—a delicate collage of feelings and failings, sadness and gladness, with happy times sparkling like sequins and crystals. We may never become a Picasso or Mozart, but our childlike picture or simple tune, our wonky pot or wobbly chair, exude the joy we felt when making them and share the integrity of masterpieces. Icing a cake, arranging flowers, cutting hair, or thatching a roof, everyone can know the elation of creation.

kiss it better

Happy hands can make a silk purse out of a sow's ear. Happy eyes search for the needle in the haystack, the hope in the bleakest situation; they look for the good in everyone, no matter what they have done or said. Some of our widest smiles in life stem from having salvaged what seemed beyond saving—from making art out of a junk-heap find. The secret of happiness is not seeking to have everything handed to us on a plate, but enjoying getting down on our knees to gather the golden crumbs under the table. Happy ears can take a sad song and make it better. Happy feet will walk to the bus stop in pouring rain and wait and wait without giving up . . . so they're there when three double-deckers come along at once.

seeds of joy

A dandelion stoically glowing in stony ground, happiness can grow in the grimmest places. Smiles can be seen and laughter heard in hospitals and hospices, numbing us to pain and facing down fears. In a prison wing, kindness and concern are keys to unlocking a padlocked heart. As that pile of pain is slowly swept away, seeds can be sown that one day will hesitantly come to flower in a chapel or a visiting room, blossoming at last in a life redeemed.

monkey business

To bring on that swinging-from-the-branches feeling, all we need to do is make like monkeys and go bananas. They are truly nature's fun-filled fruit, brimming with tryptophan, a substance that boosts our levels of serotonin, the happiness hormone. So a bountiful banana split is bound to do us good.

letting go

Something lost in the present opens up a space for something new flowing in from the future. If we hang on to happiness, fearing to let it go, it can wither before our eyes, deprived of its freedom. It is not to be netted like a butterfly and pinned down in a glass cabinet. It needs to be free as air, to rest on our shoulder, then flutter away. It will come back again if we let it go with gladness. "He who kisses the joy as it flies lives in eternity's sunrise."

go with the flow

Standing still in rushing waters takes a lot of effort. It may feel safer than letting the river of life take us where it will, but if we're too rigid and set in our ways we run the risk of missing out on happiness. It may be waiting for us downstream in a calm stretch dappled by sunlight. We're not being passive if we go with the flow—we're simply being willing, accepting all that life presents us with. We may well encounter obstacles, but if we stay flexible and fluid we will be able to pass around the rocks by the way of least resistance. "Gentleness prevails over hardness," is a mantra for happiness in Taoist philosophy.

tickling the tastebuds

What does happiness taste like? Perhaps it is a feast of fabulous yellow, of foods the color of sunshine. Bowls of happiness soup, made from lemons and yellow zucchini. Golden heaps of basmati rice infused with saffron, the herb of mirth. Crystal goblets sparkling with the zest of freshly squeezed lemonade. Fluffy omelets and canary-colored capsicums. Pineapple pieces still pulsating to a Caribbean calypso and slices of grateful grapefruit to celebrate that life is sweet.

it's in the stars

Is happiness predictable? Fortune-tellers can detect it at the
bottom of the teacup, discern it in a crystal ball or discover it
in the palm of a hopeful hand. Astrologers divine it in the complex
configurations of celestial planets and stars, rejoicing when
life-enhancing, energizing Sun and lucky, optimistic Jupiter link
up in our sign. Skeptics may take it with a pinch of salt, but
there's no harm in keeping an open mind. In happiness, often
the readiness is all.

going the extra smile

A smile is like a sacrament—an outward and visible sign of an inward invisible meaning. A smile is an instant facelift that comes from a wrinkle-free heart. Even when we are crying inside, the very act of smiling can spark the fuse that lights a Catherine wheel of happiness. A smile can launch a thousand ships laden with cargos of love. Life is made up of sobs, sniffles, and smiles. A smile and a shoeshine—all we need to walk on air. The murkiest outlook can be charmed with smiles and soap. Smiles are silk flowers embroidered on a difficult background. Bunched-up cheeks mean a smile to blind fingers. A smile is a shaft of sunlight that breaks through thick clouds to transfigure a tundra of loneliness.

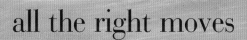

all the right moves

For yoga lovers happiness is a laid-back affair. Sadness reduces the blood supply to our brains, so a pose to restore it is a positive move. Lying on our back with arms by our sides, we bring our knees to our chest. Then we straighten our legs (as much as we can) up in the air and hold on to our toes, keeping our head on the

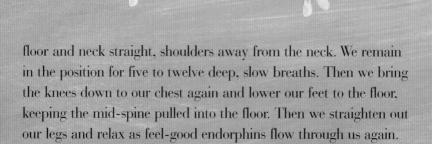

floor and neck straight, shoulders away from the neck. We remain in the position for five to twelve deep, slow breaths. Then we bring the knees down to our chest again and lower our feet to the floor, keeping the mid-spine pulled into the floor. Then we straighten out our legs and relax as feel-good endorphins flow through us again.

scents of occasion

Just one whiff of coconut oil and we're back in a blissful beach cabana, limbo-dancing to reggae and greeting a tequila sunrise. A fig-fragranced candle carries us to a terracotta terrace and a mouthful of summer succulence. New-mown grass replays that moment in a baseball game when we made a jaw-dropping, jubilant catch. Beeswax brings back grandmother's cottage, pine the glee of a Christmas stocking. Our sense of smell can suffuse us with smiling memories, as it is linked directly to the part of our brain that governs remembrance, instincts, and emotions. And a cut-glass bottle of amber liquid can hold the essence of happiness. Our signature scent is a droplet of distilled delight, for our perfume is our shadow, our inner self: the identity card of our spirit. To find it is to have forever a sparkling-stoppered source of pure joy.

treasure trove

A collection of favorite things can become our happiness shrine. A private corner filled with beautiful objects that have special meaning for us refreshes our soul when we spend a little time there every day, simply resting and reflecting. It may feature tokens of our deepest beliefs—a crucifix, icons, rosary beads, or a Buddha; a statuette of Ganesa, the Hindu elephant god of new beginnings and removing obstacles, with a picture of Durga, goddess of wisdom and learning. Or it may represent the people and places that mean the most to us: photographs of family, friends, and inspiring people; postcards recalling happy holidays; little treasures collected over time, such as pebbles, buttons, shells, and souvenirs; rose quartz stone for love and healing; candles or a string of fairy lights, flowers, or an incense stick. It can be colorful and kitsch if our character is kooky, or minimal and calm if we're more composed—as long as it expresses who we are, centers us, and replenishes our hearts with happiness.

moving on

R ainbow happiness is the radiance we feel
when we realize we can redeem the past.
However much we have sabotaged our lives, we can
start afresh and build something beautiful. Our
characters are not carved in stone: we can remake
ourselves, become the new self we want to be. We can
see our past as a dusty cellar, piled with trunks full of

experiences. They will always be there, but we can make one
final visit, lifting lids and remembering, then closing them all and
coming out and locking the door. When we take responsibility for
all that is there, but learn from it and resolve to move on, the
mistakes of yesterday become the wisdom of tomorrow. Life
stretches before us as a poppy field of possibility. We can stretch
out sun-kissed arms and run toward it with rapture.

moment of truth

It can happen to any one of us, not just Pythagoras: that marvelous eureka moment. We can scratch our heads for days on end trying to solve a crucial problem, but the answer teases and tantalizes us, just beyond our fingertips. The words we want for the very last line, the notes we need for the final chord, are out there in the shadows somewhere. We tremble on the brink of a breakthrough but cannot make that leap in the dark. Then suddenly the light bulb goes on in our head. It happens at the oddest moments, when we're washing the dishes or walking the dog or bowling along in an open-topped car over hills alive with our favorite tune. The answer is dizzily, dazzlingly lovely and the world becomes one glorious gorgeous glitterball.

invitation to the waltz

Happiness is the perfect dancing partner. It lifts us high in a pas de deux and flirts with us in a flamenco. It never treads on our toes and is never routine. It whirls us around in a dizzying waltz and high-kicks with us in a cancan. It teaches us to sway to the rhythm of life and dance to the music of time. It leaves us solo from time to time on an empty and shadowy stage, but its steps are imprinted in our memories so we can still be a dancer in the dark. When it reappears again from the wings it will take us to trip the light fantastic.

level best

If we were all high fliers, there wouldn't be anyone to do the essential groundwork. Happiness flows from being ourselves and finding our own level. Often we strain to live up to the great expectations that others have of us, or to ones we pile on ourselves. At work we may be promoted above the glass ceiling but find it a slippery place to be, and gaze down longingly at

our old niche where we felt we belonged. We don't have to be in the limelight if we're happiest behind the scenes or dive from the top platform if we're best on the springboard. It is more important to focus on who we want to be than what we want to achieve. The key thing is to reach the rung on the ladder that is right for us—that is our happy medium.

teamwork

Happiness is a game of two halves. When we feel on the ball, good things seem to head in our direction and there is simply no stopping us. We tackle problems with practiced skill and achieve impossible goals. We cherish the camaraderie of teamwork, of striving with others to get a result. Then something happens to spoil it. We feel as if we are paying a penalty for everything going so well before. Or we bring disappointment on ourselves and know we have only ourselves to blame. We think it's all over. It is then that a different kind of happiness kicks in—the kind that comes when friends rally round to support us, and no one blames us for scoring on our own goal. There is no substitute for that.

don't hurry, be happy

Multitasking 24/7, hurtling toward a receding horizon, we end up burned out, not blissed out. Zappy rarely equals happy. Accelerating faster than the speed of life, we feel we are spinning out of control. But by slowing down to a snail's pace we can sense our stresses slipping away and a blissful peace taking their place. Zen "mindfulness" soothes our soul and blesses us with a timeless tranquillity. It is the wisdom of total absorption in what we are doing, giving all our attention to the present. We can learn it in restful activities like t'ai chi and tapestry, then extend it to every task we do. Thoughts come and go in our mind but we remain calmly focused, endowing the single task with value: we find significance in the smallest things, so that "what is little becomes much." In mindfulness we are fully ourselves, as our innermost spirit silently unfurls. Treasuring each new-made moment, we are not pulled two ways by the past and the future. Happiness is the simple loveliness of a still life.

life is beautiful

If we don't demand gifts of life but just love it for itself, we always feel that what we are given is far too much and overflow with thankfulness. Contentment comes from feeling that enough is enough. From taking nothing for granted. We are not always longing to walk on water, for we realize that the miracle is being able to walk at all. Happiness is relative: to a gymnast it is a body that bends beyond belief; to a paraplegic it is feeling a pinprick or being able to blink an eyelid. Possessions can make us feel possessed, compelled to pursue the next big thing. Simplicity imparts serenity; we hear angel voices in a tiny shell and a rosebud gives a glimpse of heaven.

water of life

Happiness is Minnehaha, laughing water, a tumbling cascade of merriment. It bursts out in the burble, the gurgle, the ripple of a giggle. Happiness is a softly splashing fountain of youth in a wise old heart. Guilt for something we have done or said can be like a hard boulder in the middle of a stream, gathering all our other failings around it and damming the natural flow of our being. But confession sweeps the rock downstream and joy courses through us, crystal clear. Happiness is vast and awesome as the oceans, yet after a drought it is precious as liquid gold, cupped in our hands so as not to lose a drop.

lighten up, brighten up

It's fine to like to feel in control, but being a control freak is not much fun. Sometimes we need to lighten up and let someone else take the controls. They can teach us how to fly by the seat of our pants for a change and feel that life's a breeze. Being an airhead can make us lighthearted. It's good to care about getting things right, but obsessions can obstruct the way to happiness. If we hold on tight to the bee in our bonnet, there can't be any honey for tea.

once in a while

Things don't have to happen for us to feel happy—sometimes it's enough that they don't happen. Once in a while the toast doesn't fall on the buttered side, tights don't snag, and the 8:22 train isn't delayed. Test results come back all clear and car wheels pass around the hedgehog. In a seething sea the ship doesn't sink,

while on dry land the harvest doesn't
fail. A hurtful comment we would
always regret is held back behind sealed lips.
A little bare foot limps over a landmine, too light to make
it detonate. A nation on the brink holds back from war.

ups and downs

Life is a fairground merry-go-round. We ride on gaily painted horses and hear the hurdy-gurdy music. Sometimes we rise high above the crowds and wave at our friends below, then we drop down for a while. But it isn't long before we are whisked up again and feel on top of the world. We are bound to experience ups and downs; everyone meets with setbacks, disappointments, and rejection. But if we keep holding on to hope we will in time be lifted up again and smile at the future spread out before us.

First published by MQ Publications Limited
12 The Ivories, 6–8 Northampton Street
London N1 2HY

Copyright © 2003 MQ Publications Limited

TEXT COPYRIGHT © 2003 **libby willis**
DESIGN CONCEPT: **balley design associates**

ISBN: 0-7407-3868-2

Library of Congress Control Number: 2003103013